I0485586

Enchanted Love

The Mandala Coloring book

By

S.B. Nozaz

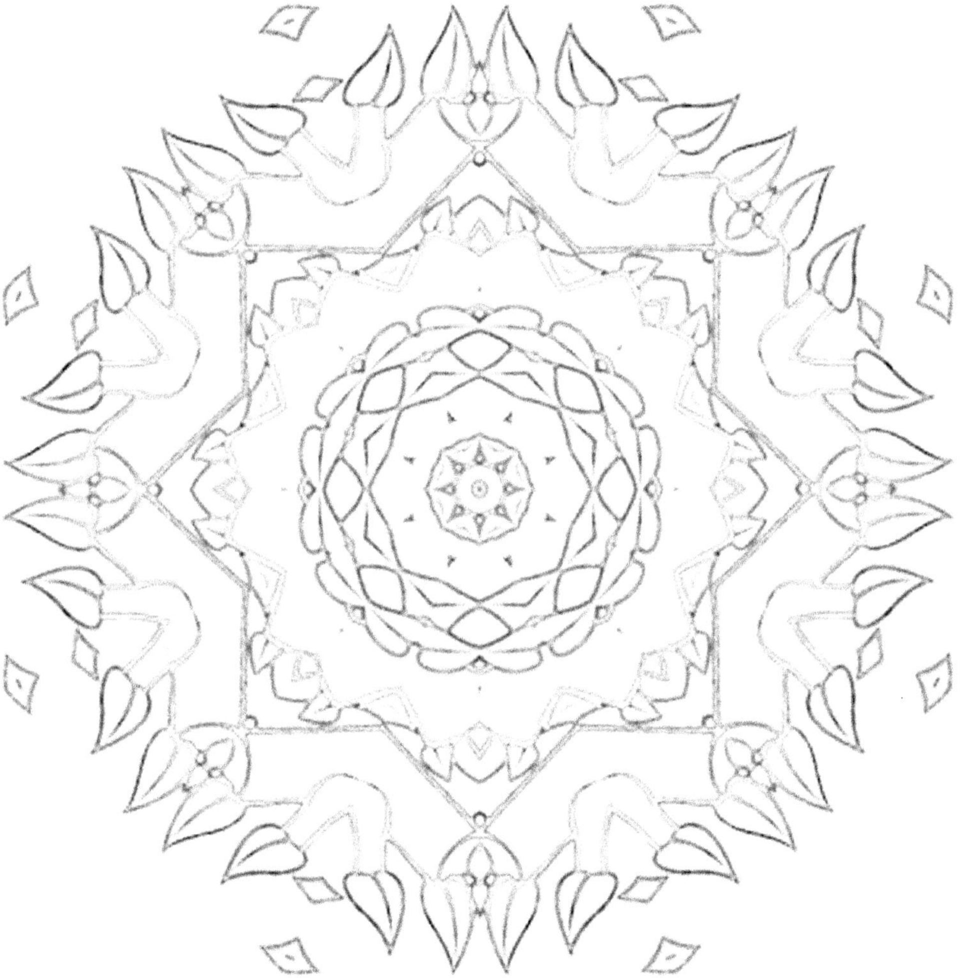

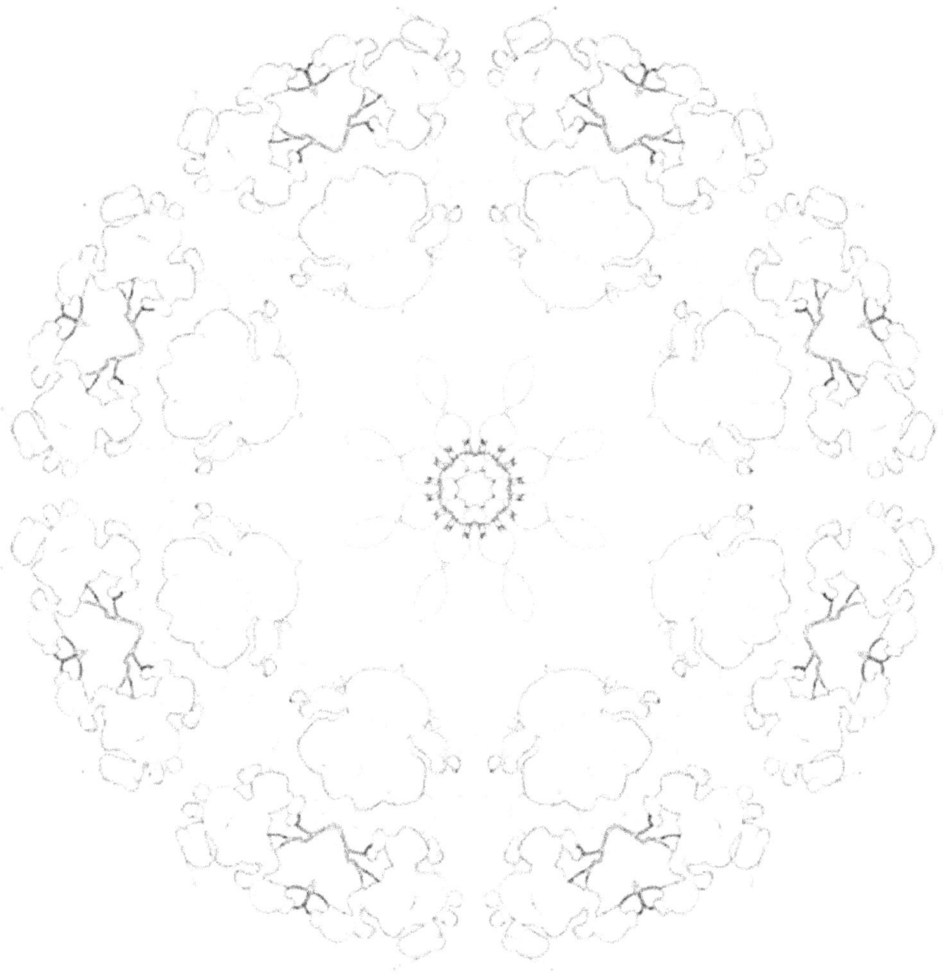

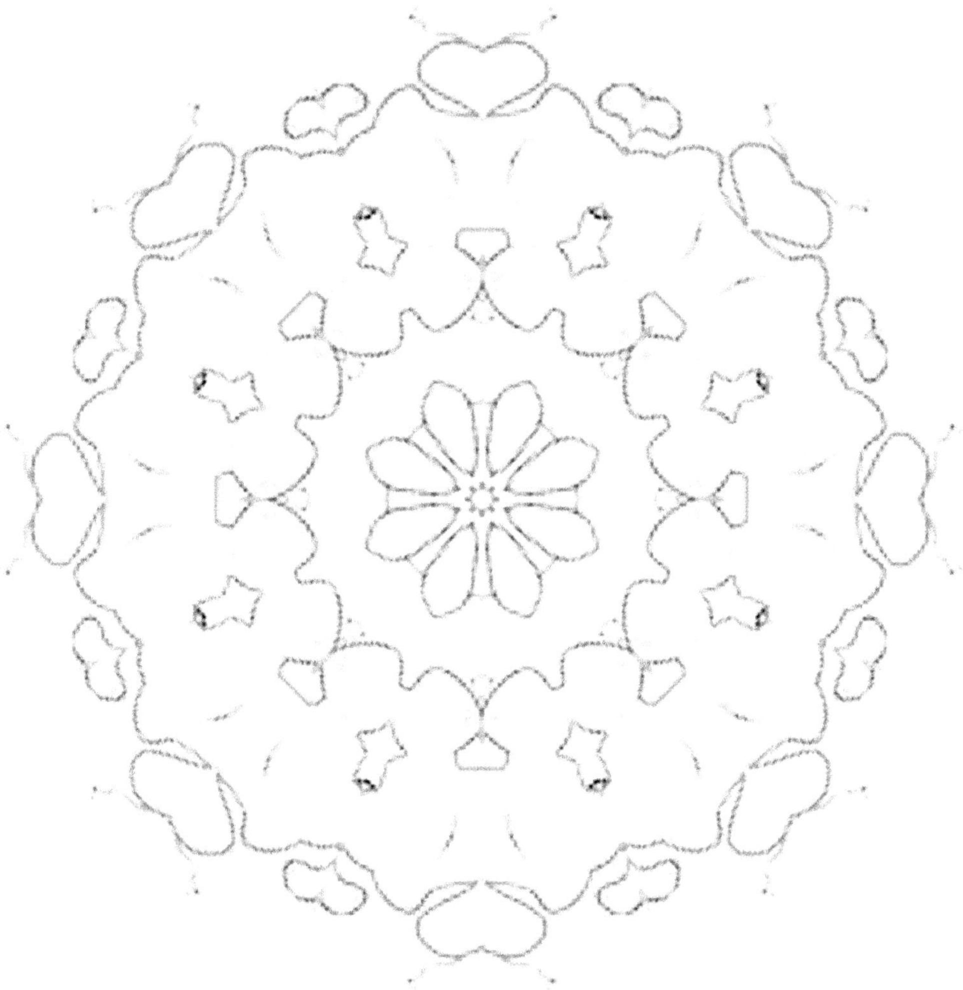

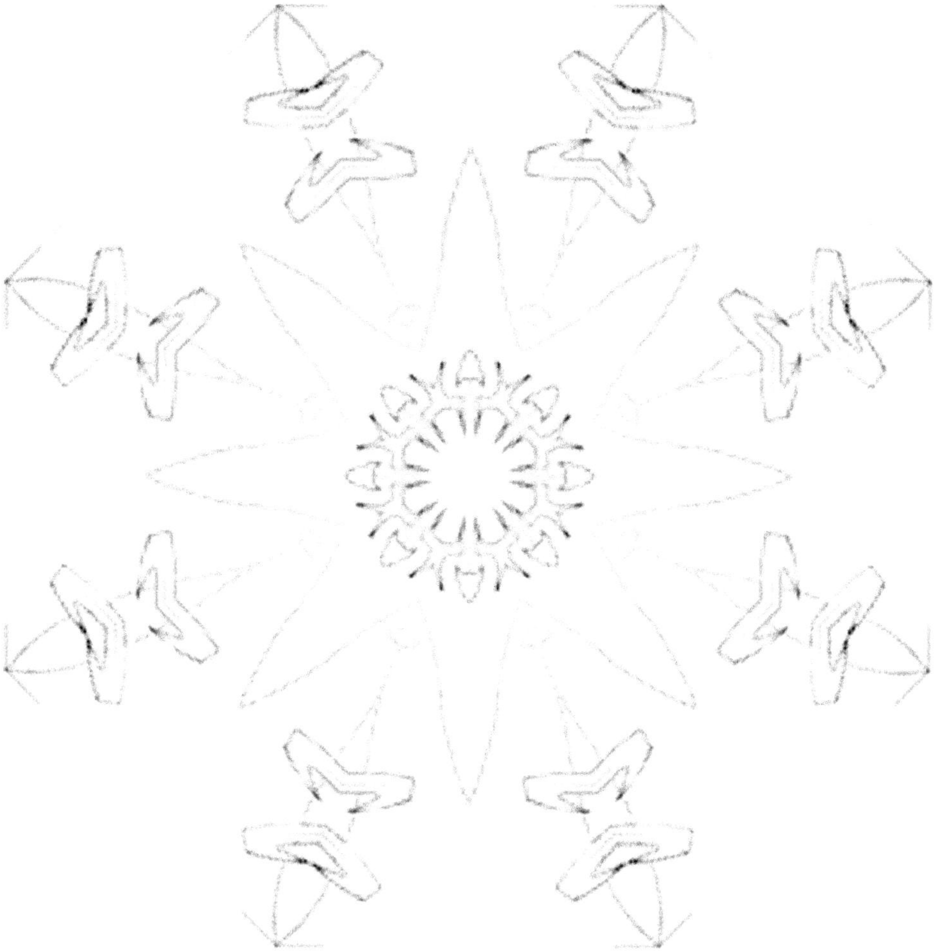

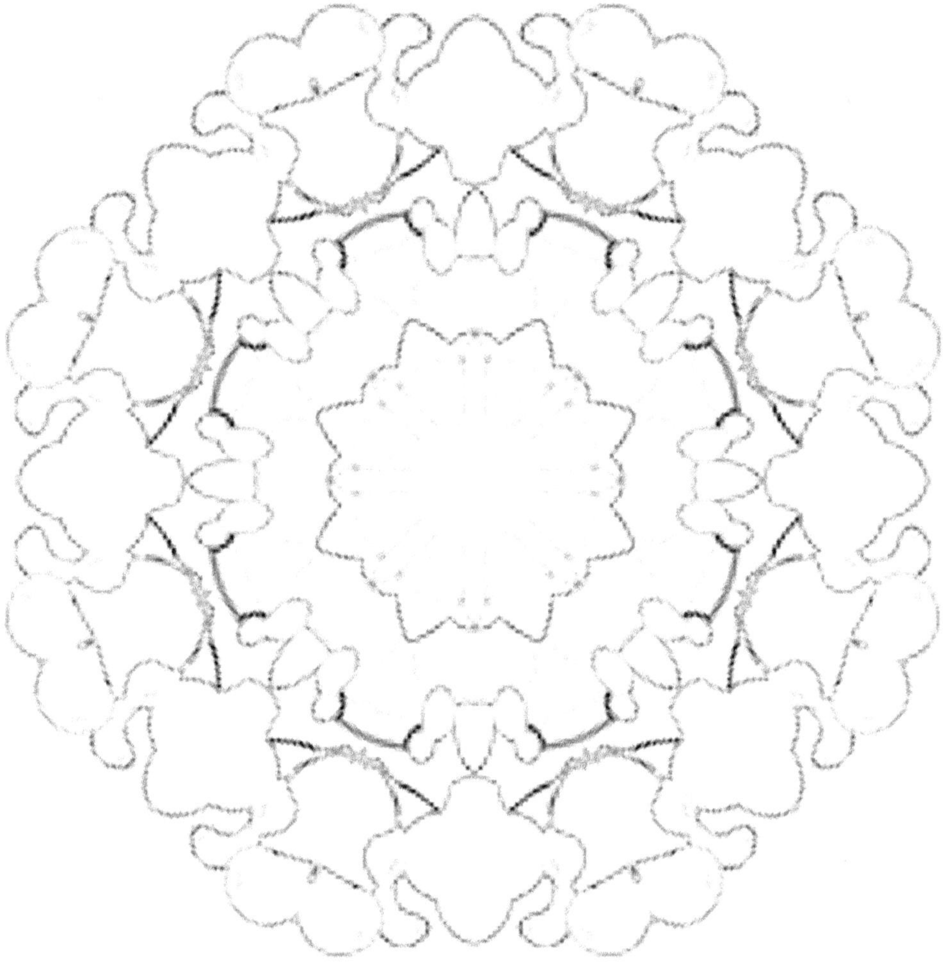

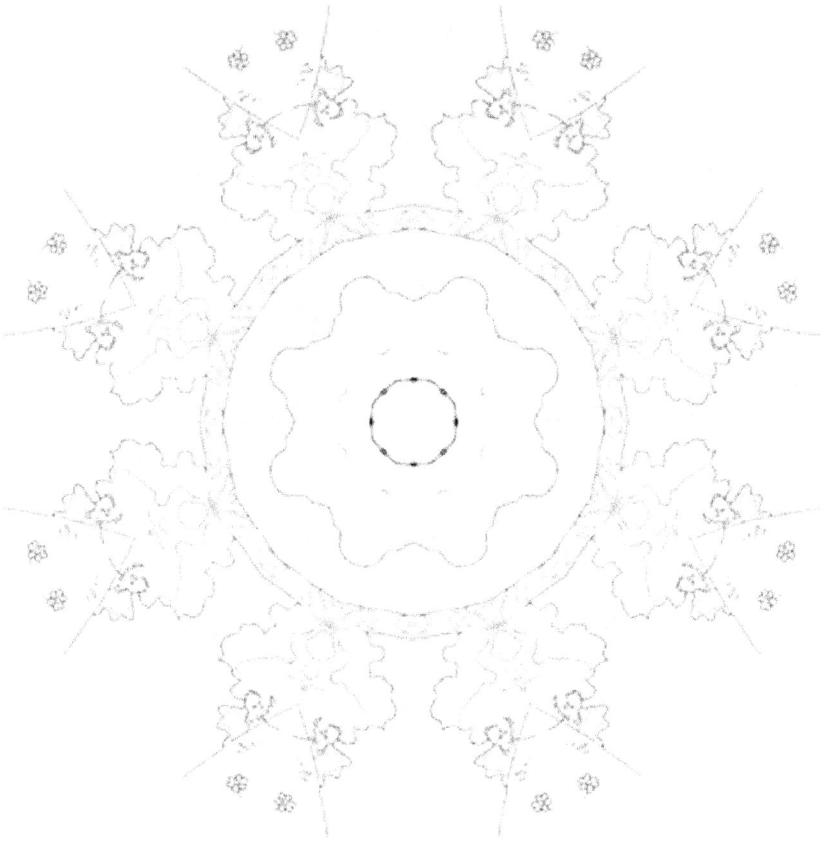

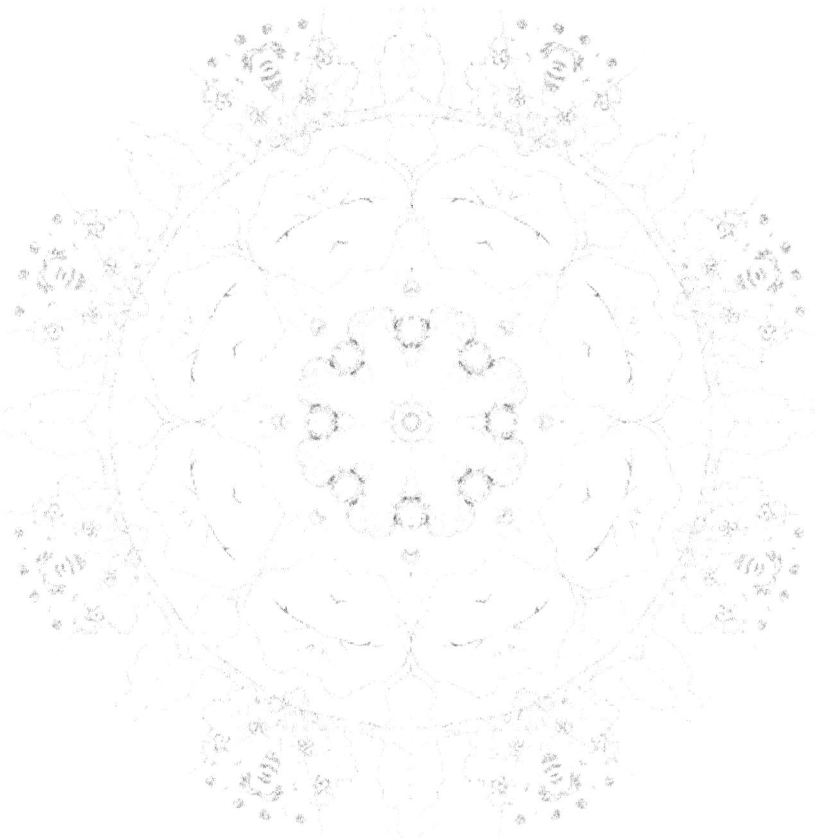

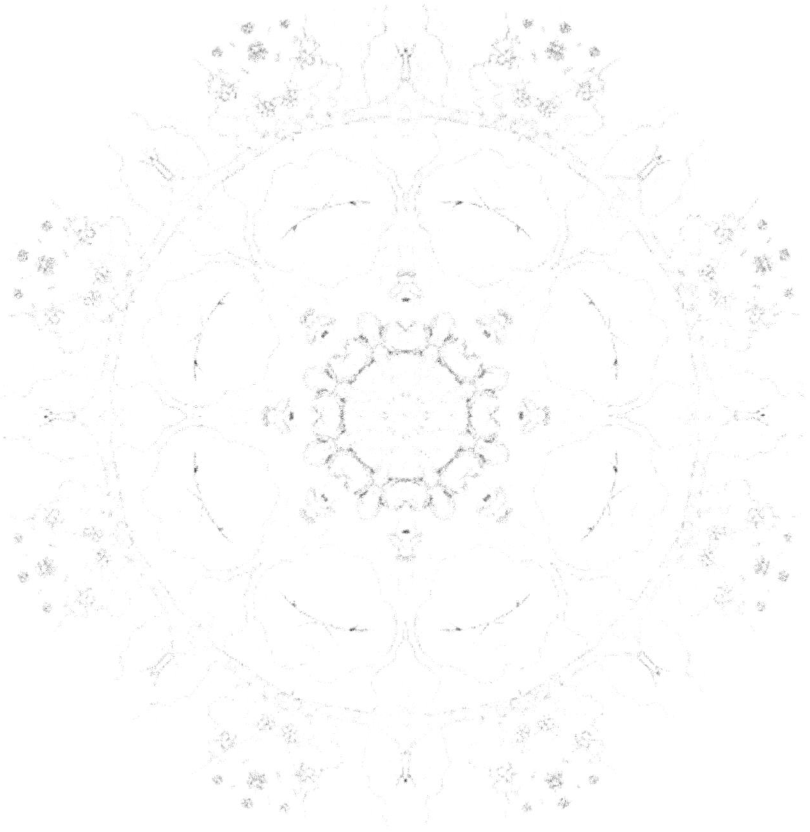

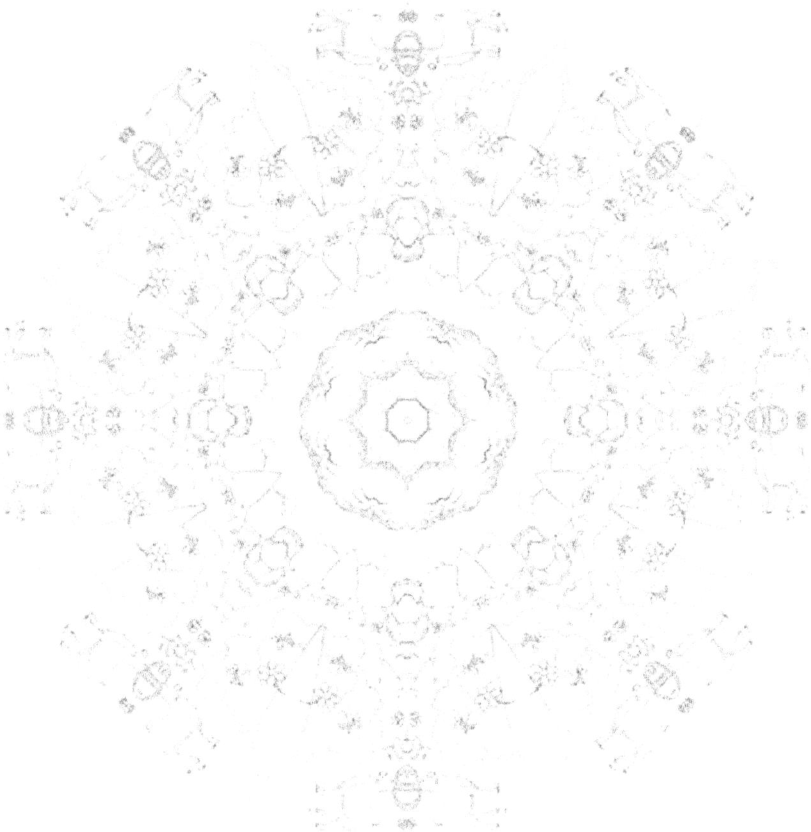

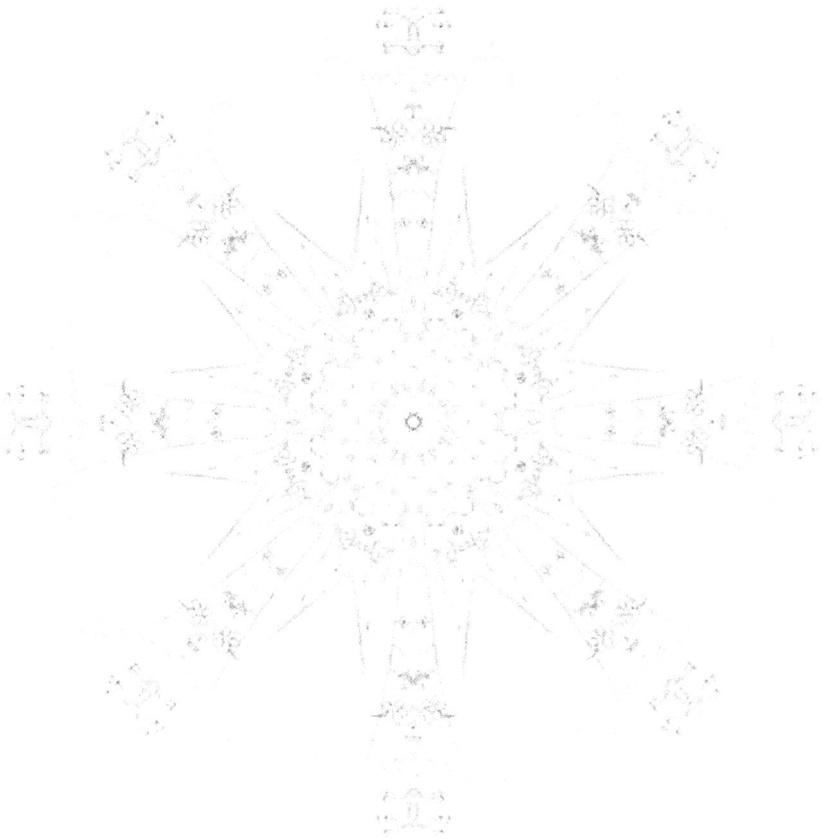

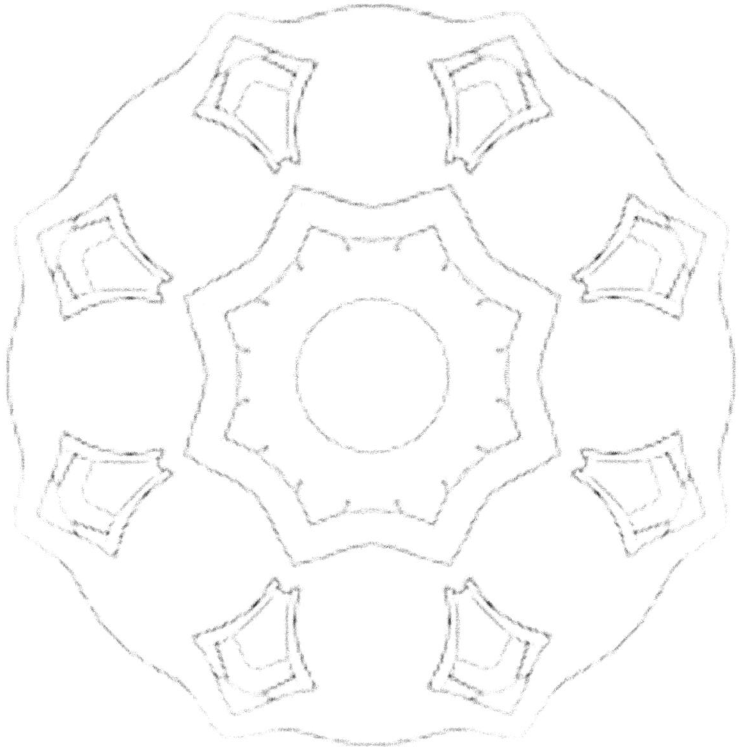

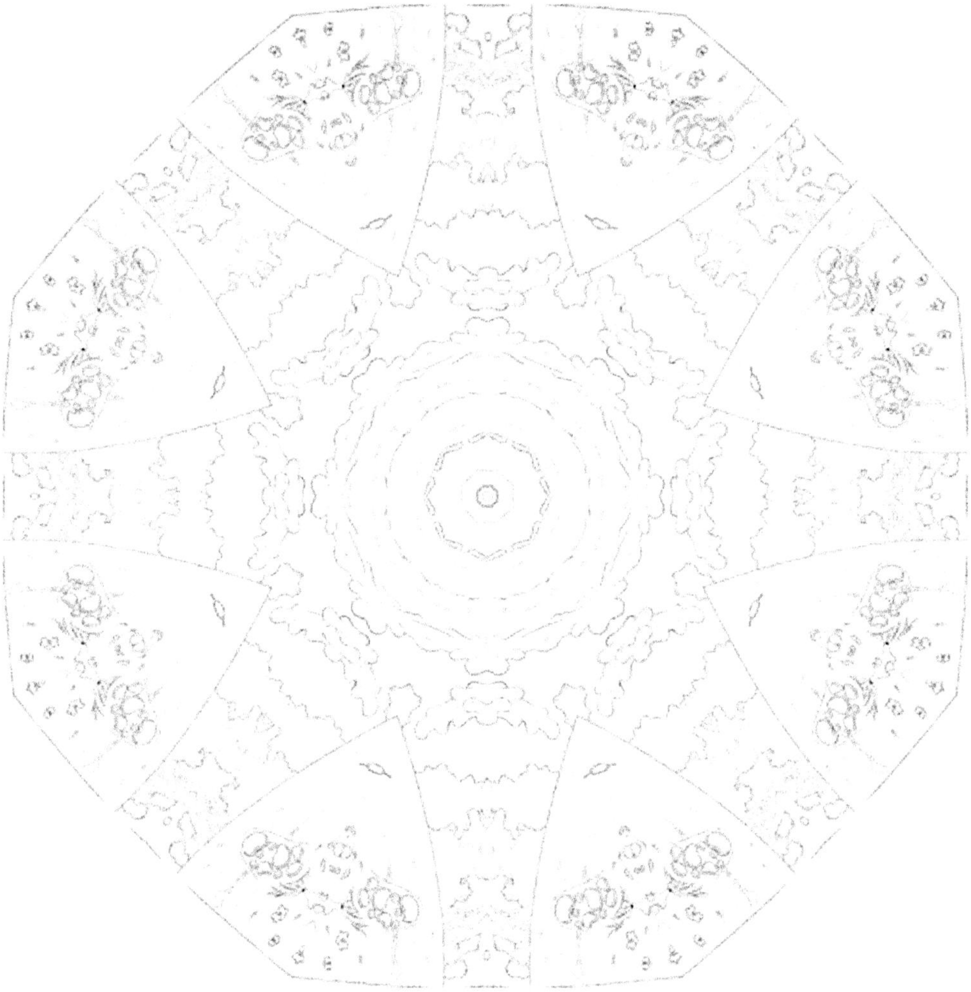

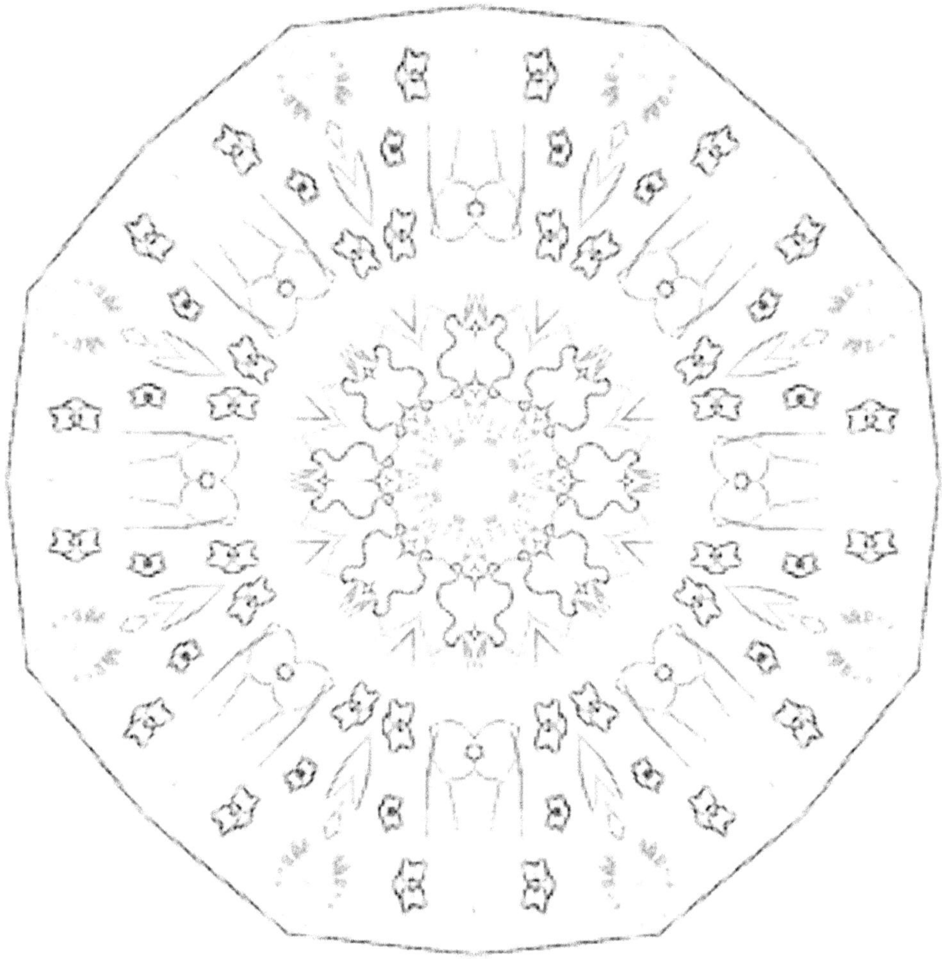

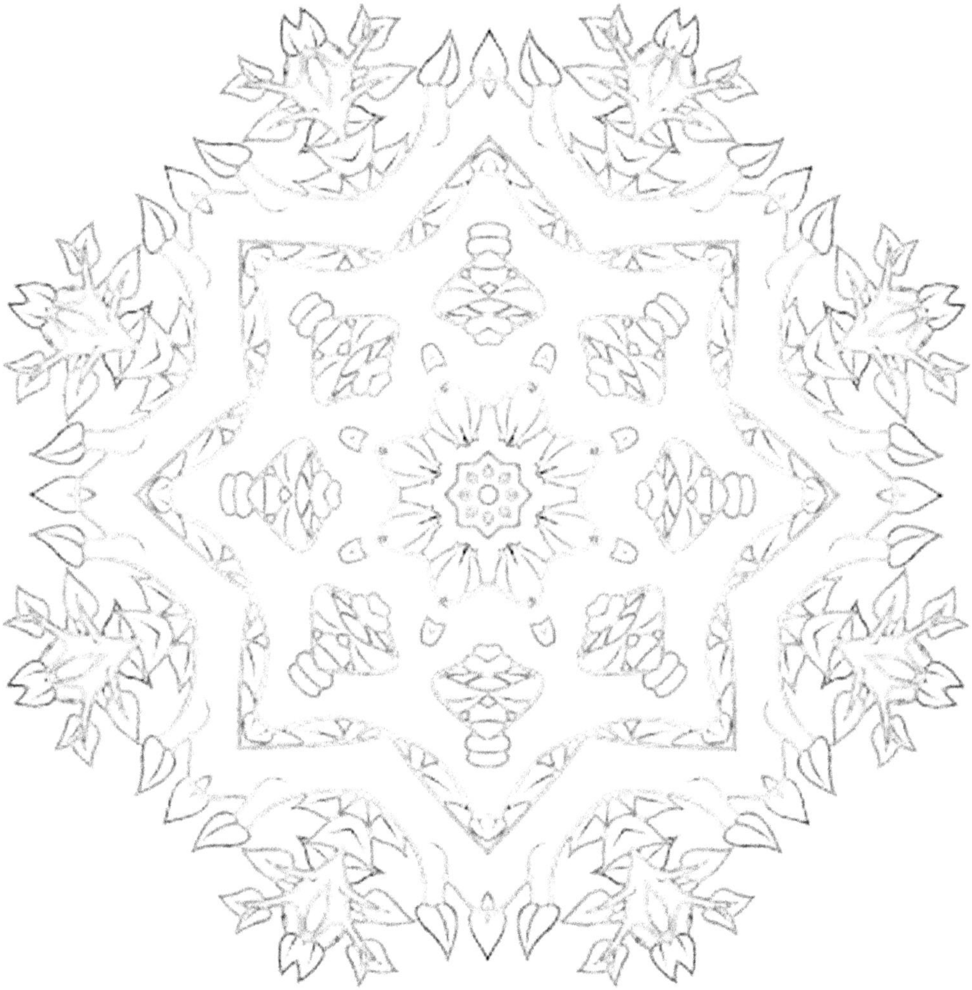

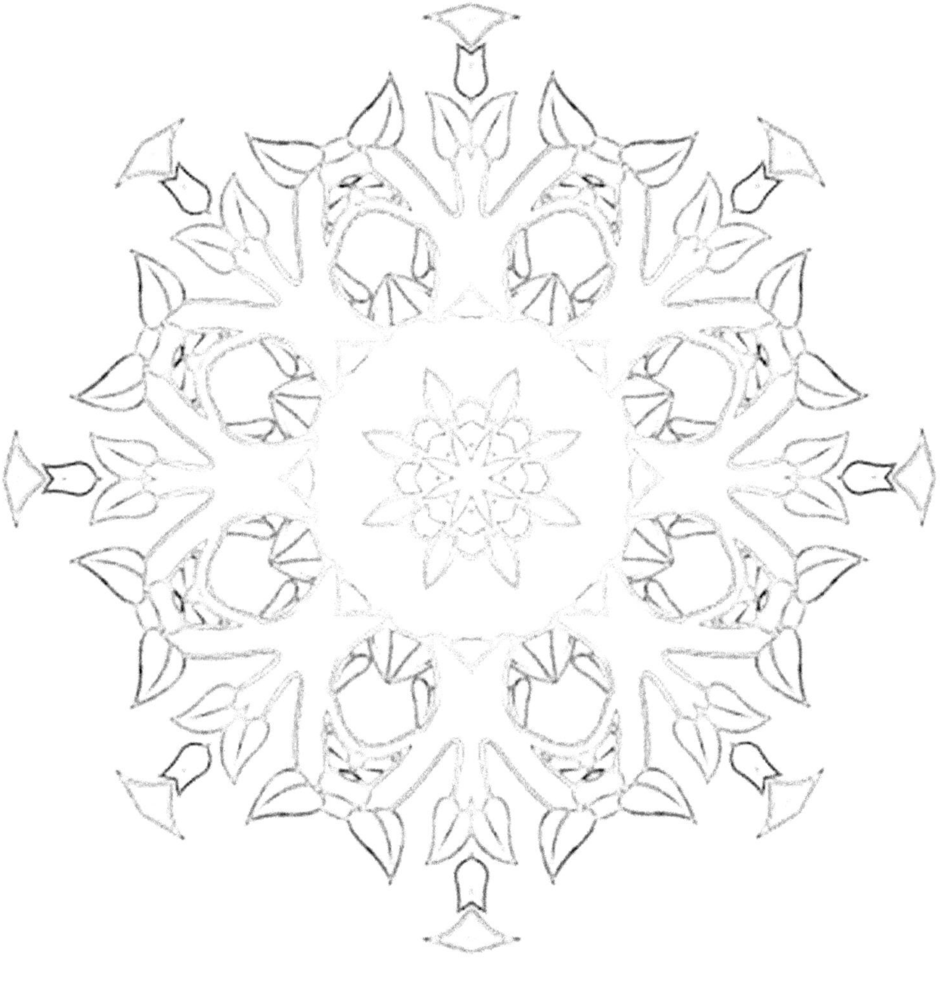

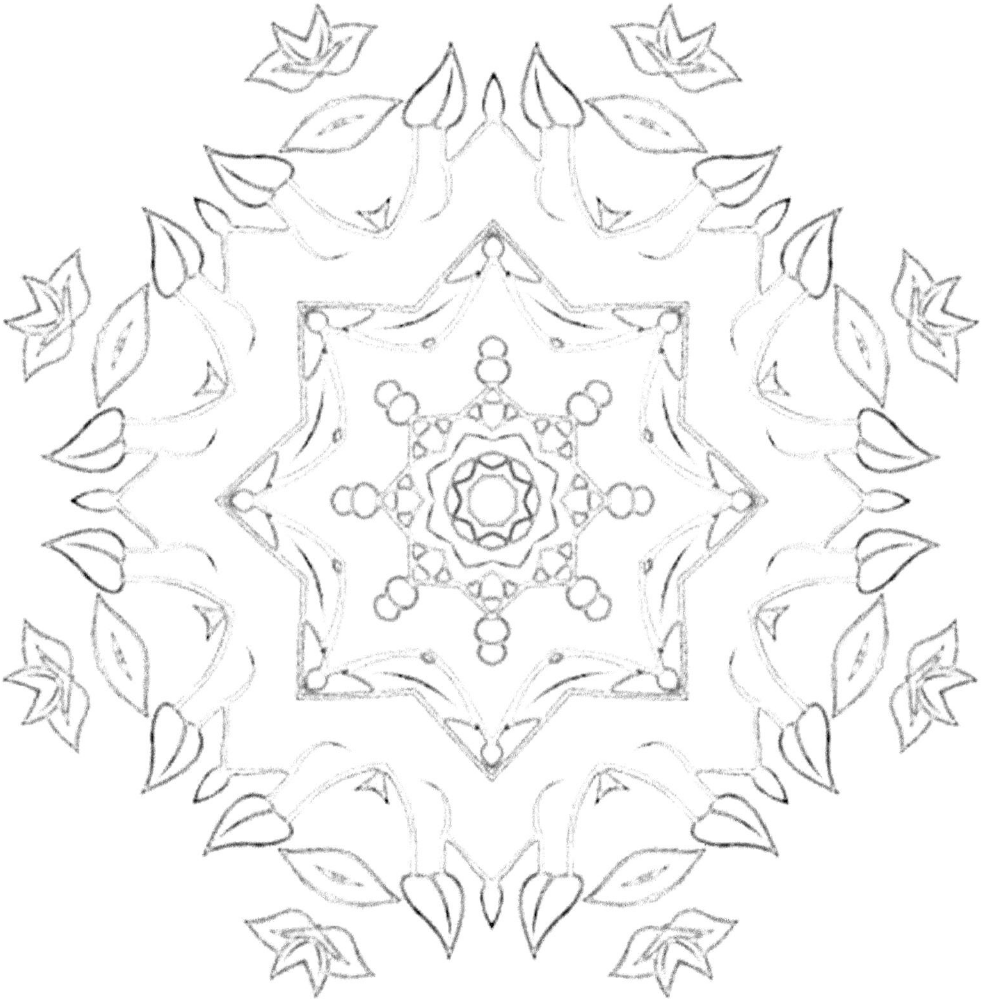

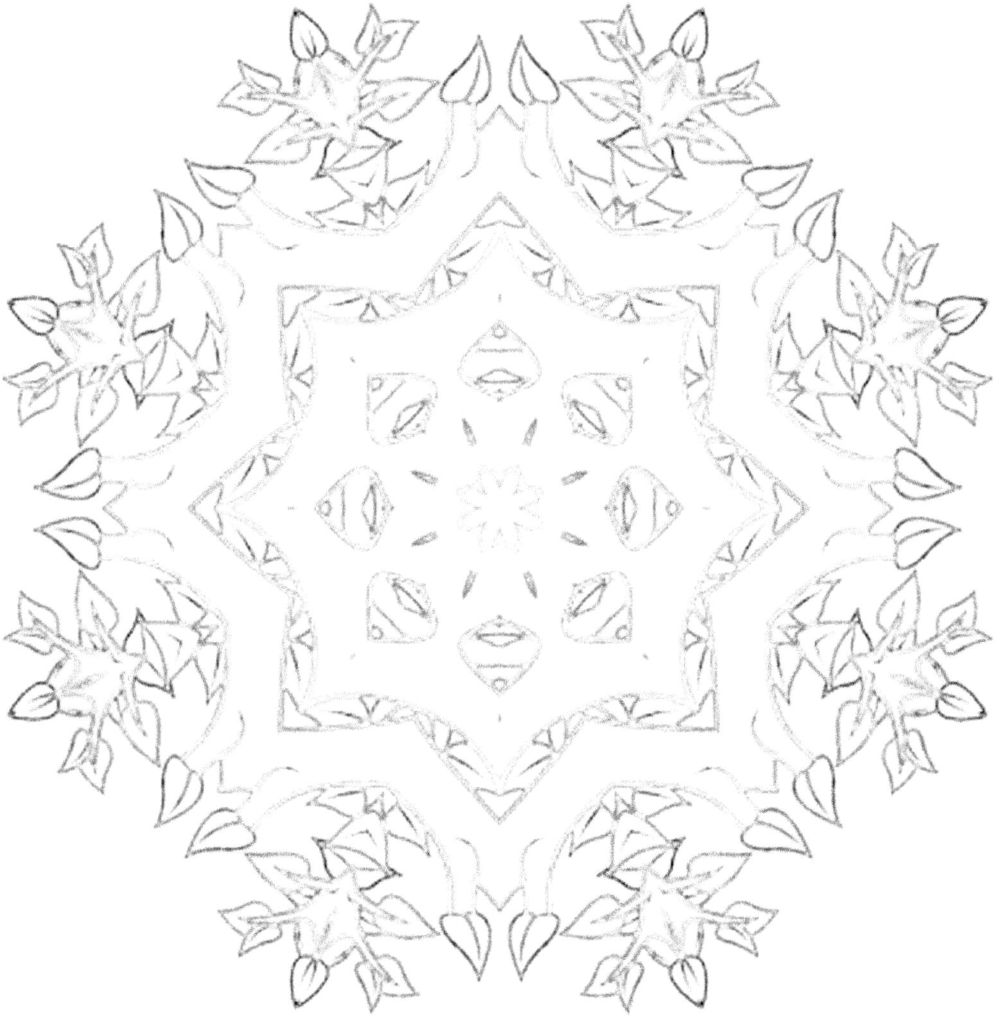

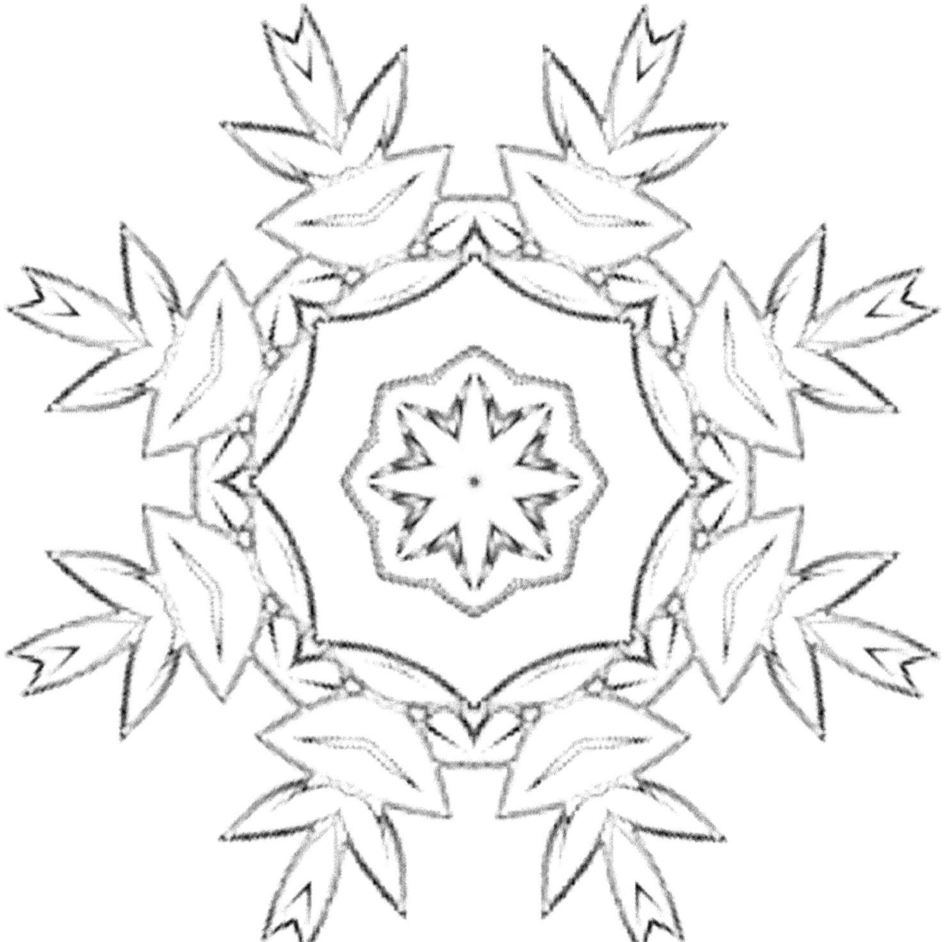

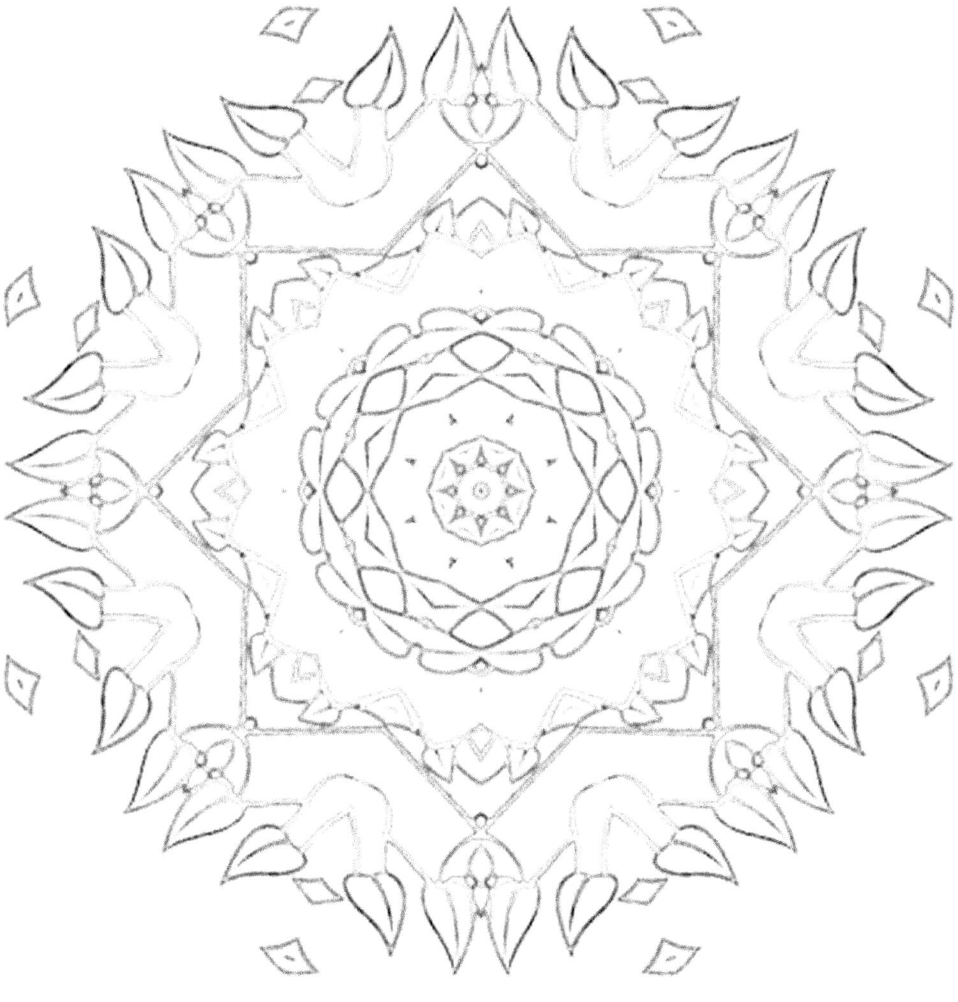

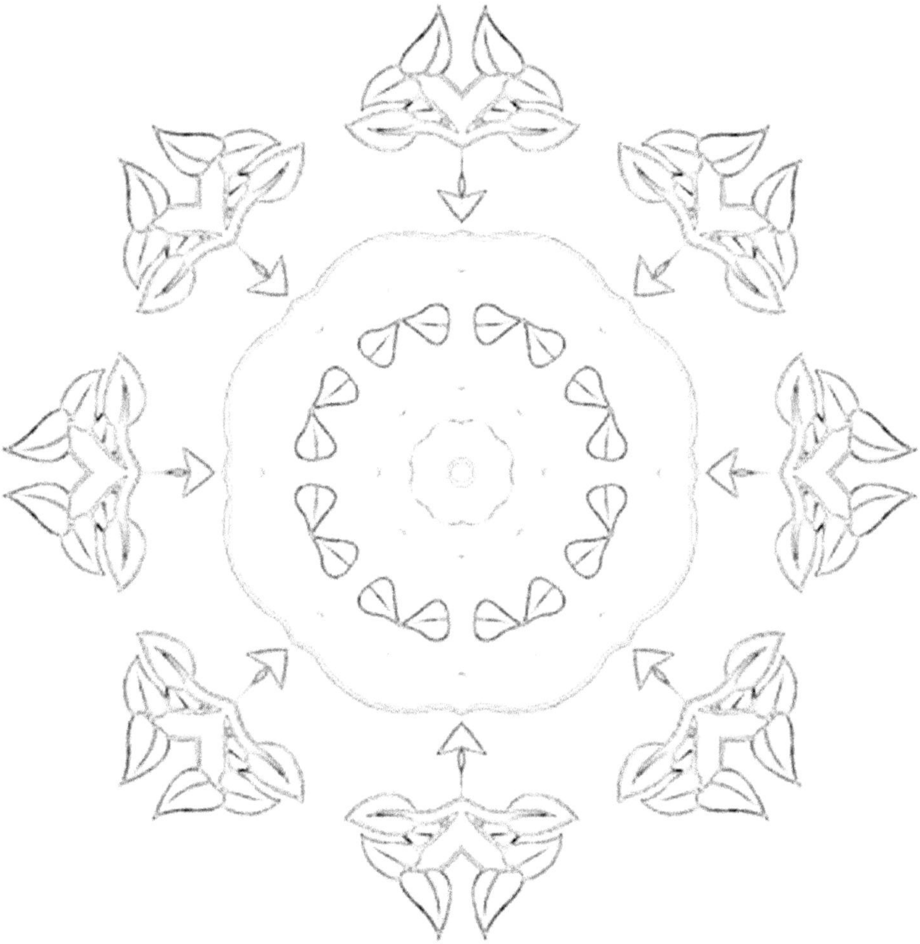

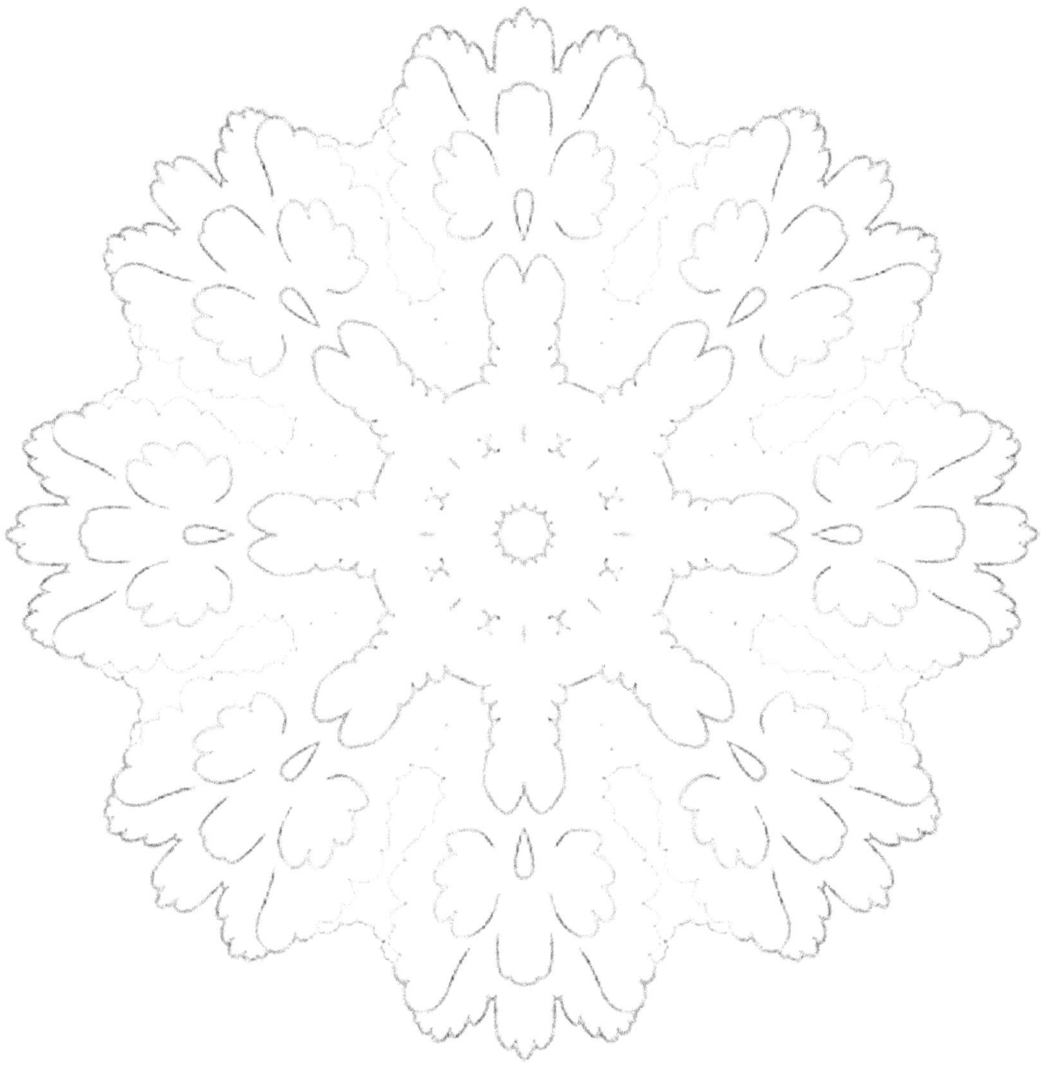

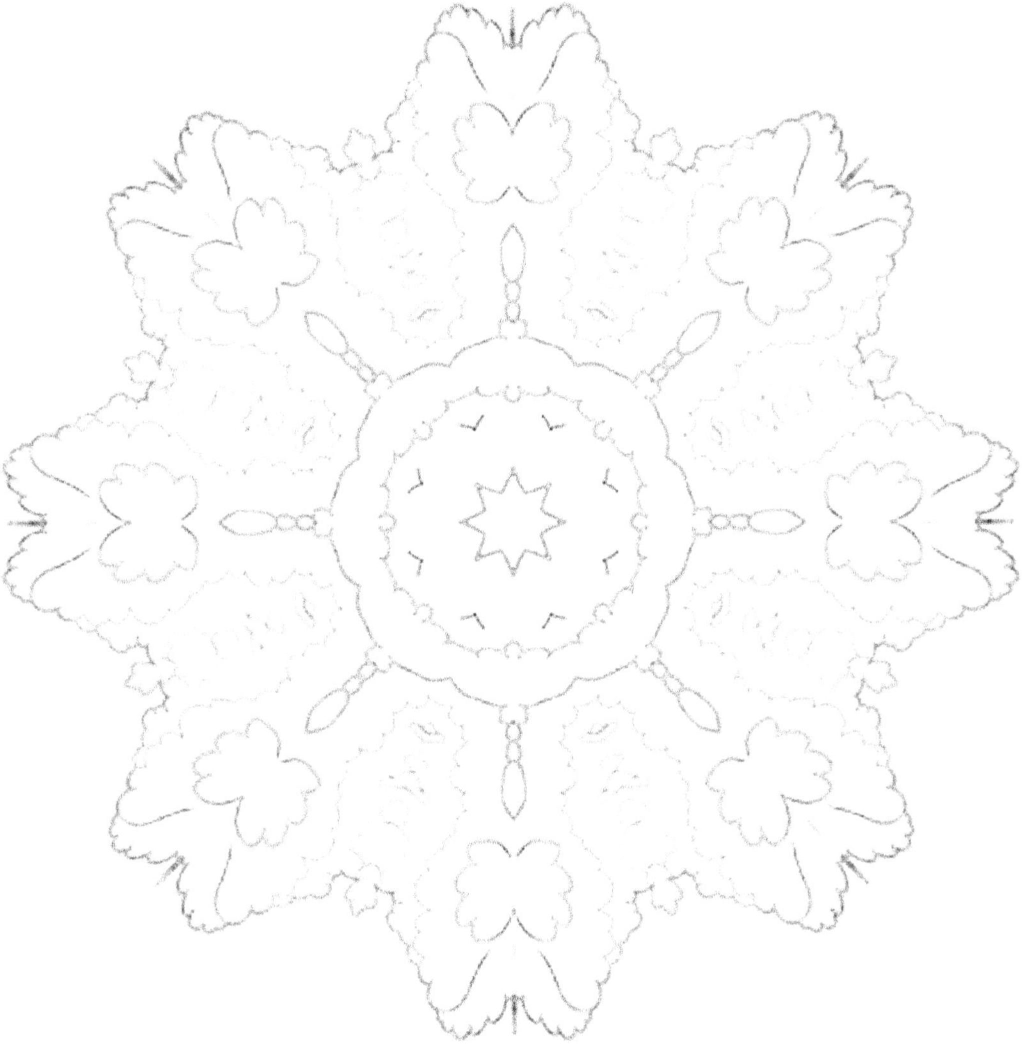

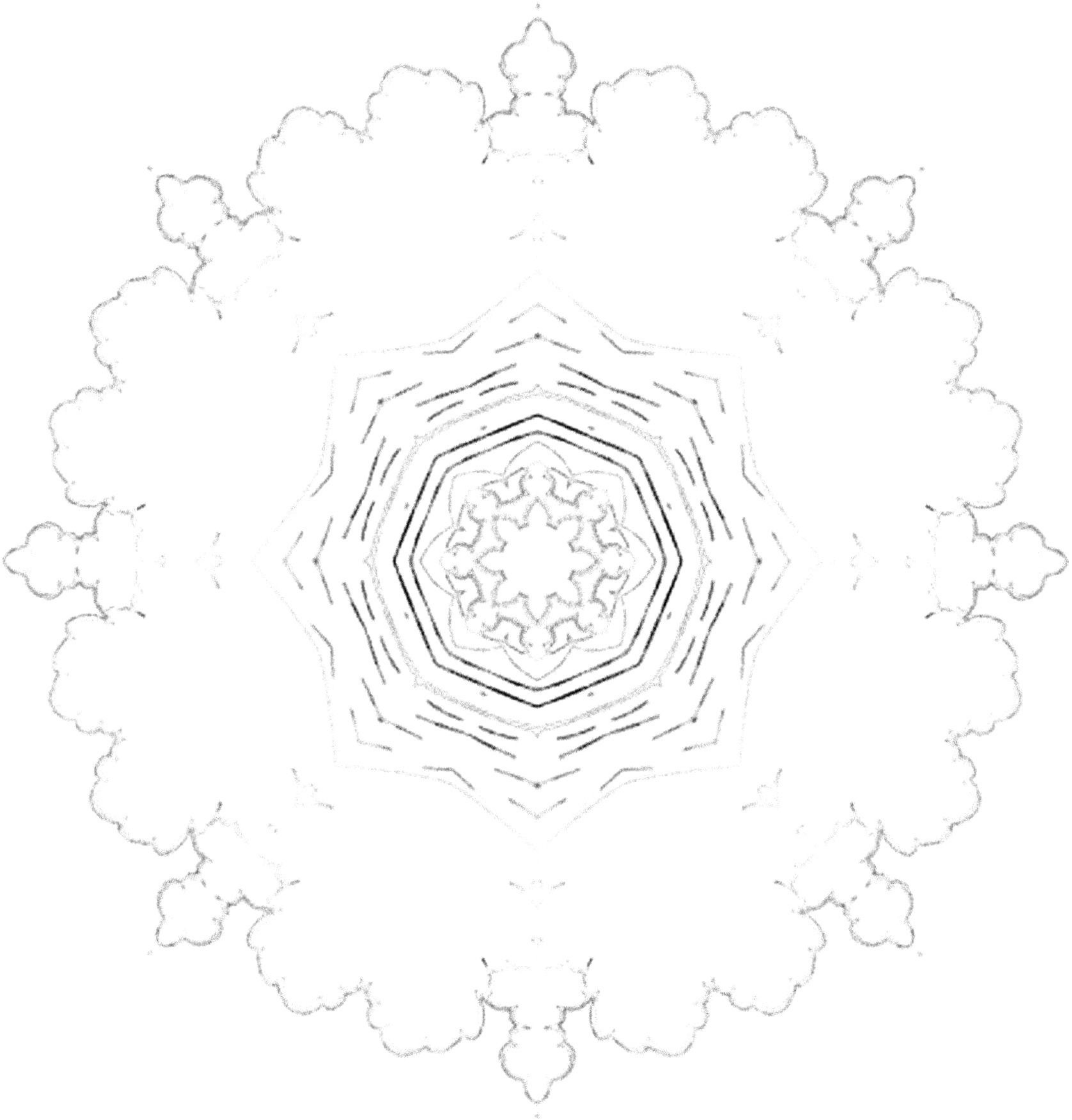

Note

www.ingramcontent.com/pod-product-compliance
Lightning Source LLC
Chambersburg PA
CBHW080649180526
45168CB00008B/3351
9781517471781